AMAZON PLANS OF ACTION
Proven Tactics for Winning Appeals

SCOTT MARGOLIUS

Copyright © 2021 Scott Margolius

All rights reserved.

PRAISE FOR *AMAZON PLANS OF ACTION*

This book is easy to read, easy to apply, and genuinely helpful. If you want to have a better chance of being reinstated or winning a case, read it. Every Amazon seller should have this in their tool kit or they risk costly mistakes.

--Steven Yates, former Amazon executive and Founder of Prime Guidance

In order to have staying power as a business on the largest ecommerce platform on the planet, you HAVE TO learn how to successfully appeal cases. There is no way around it. Finally, someone has given sellers a fighting chance…in the form of the principles in *Amazon Plans of Action: Proven Tactics for Winning Appeals*.

--Ed Rosenberg, Founder of ASGTG.com

Scott Margolius uses examples and clear writing to answer the perennial question: "What does Amazon want?!?" By explaining the thought process behind an appeal, his book helps sellers feel confident to tackle a wide range of suspension challenges. It is an asset to the seller community.

--Cynthia Stine, Founder of eGrowthPartners.com

Scott Margolius is a trusted name in the Amazon consulting space for a reason. He consistently delivers for sellers when they are in the most dire of situations. *Amazon Plans of Action* is vital, concise, and practical. It has everything you need to navigate the murky waters of the Amazon appeal process.

--Jim Cockrum, Founder SilentJim.com and ProvenAmazonCourse.com

Amazon Plans of Action is a much-needed book for any and all Amazon sellers, no matter their experience level, sales history, or monthly revenues. Scott walks people through how to win an appeal with Amazon. Great book from a great consultant and great guy. I really couldn't recommend it more. If you sell on Amazon, get this book!

--Nate McCallister, Entreresource.com and Founder of FBA Today

DEDICATION

To my family, friends, and all of the hard-working sellers who deserve a break...

CONTENTS

	INTRODUCTION	1
I.	THE CURRENT CRISIS IS A CATALYST	5
II.	WHY PLANS OF ACTION ARE SO COMMON	11
III.	WHAT IS A PLAN OF ACTION?	17
IV.	FOUNDATIONAL RESEARCH: DETECTIVE WORK AS THE FIRST STEP TO WINNING YOUR APPEAL	25
V.	FINAL CONSIDERATIONS BEFORE WRITING	35
VI.	IT'S FINALLY TIME…TO WRITE	41
VII.	COMMON MISTAKES AND POST SUBMISSION SUGGESTIONS	53
VIII.	FINAL CHECKLIST	63
	GLOSSARY	69

ACKNOWLEDGMENTS

The author would like to acknowledge the business owners he has been able to help along the way. You have helped him as much as he has helped you…

INTRODUCTION

I realize that a majority of people who come to this book are in a state of concern, or even panic. Most likely, you sought this book out because of a problem with your Amazon seller account. Chances are good you received a communication from Amazon which requires you to submit a Plan of Action in order to continue selling a particular ASIN or ASINs, or to continue selling on Amazon in general.

I am here to tell you that what you are going through is very common. And no matter how it may feel at the moment, keep in mind the majority of sellers are able to fix these types of problems. You came to the right place. I have been helping sellers with appeals and Account Health concerns for many years now, and I can say from experience that most problems are able to be resolved. Let me repeat this: no matter what you are facing, the chances are very, very good you will be able to continue selling on Amazon. In fact, chances are very good, if you apply the principles in this guide, that you will reach a new level of success with your account.

There is hope. All is not lost. *The chances are in your favor.*

This book is specifically written to help sellers strategize and write successful Plans of Action. What you are reading is the culmination, knowledge, and experience of hundreds of successful appeals for sellers just like you, who came to me in a state of desperation, thinking that their businesses were about to end. Almost every single client I have worked with to write a POA has had their issue(s) resolved in a satisfactory manner. And we will fix your issues, together, as well!

AMAZON PLANS OF ACTION

In the pages that follow I am going to give you a crash course in Plans of Action (POAs). We will begin with your attitude, then examine research, then common mistakes, and then, finally, the actual writing process. In addition, I am also going to help you with preparing invoices, where/how to submit your finished plan, and then take a look at how to avoid the need for future POAs. We are going to discuss the real root cause of your issues, looking at your business structure as a whole, to address the *reasons* Amazon requests Plans of Action. We are going to look at this process from every necessary angle to give you everything you need to win your appeals.

Everything is going to be ok, provided you approach the pages that follow with an open mind, and a hopeful attitude. If you are willing to do these two things, reading through this guide should feel light, easy, and refreshing. I realize, when problems occur, you naturally feel anything but *light*. But, I am confident that your POA request can serve as an opportunity for growth as a seller, rather than a hindrance or a burden. As you read through the pages that follow, you should come away more confident, and much better equipped.

Believe that good things are coming, because they are!

SCOTT MARGOLIUS

AMAZON PLANS OF ACTION

I. THE CURRENT CRISIS IS A CATALYST

Disneyland is always a great idea. Well, *almost* always.

It was late January, 2020. The holiday season was just wrapping up. Alex was planning a sourcing trip to Disney to pick up some merchandise to resell on his Amazon store, as he had several times in the months prior. This last trip to the park (prior to its closing due to the global pandemic) would prove to be a unique one, to say the least.

Alex had been hearing rumors of a new sickness that was spreading quickly in several countries across the globe. Like many others at that point in time, he was not taking the threats seriously, as not many were yet referring to it as a pandemic. He certainly didn't consider a visit to Disneyland to be potentially hazardous to his health. There were voices of warning in the media at that point, but he thought…*there's no way that Coronavirus will affect ME*. Caution was not on his mind, and he didn't even consider wearing a mask or carrying hand sanitizer.

He made his rounds in the park, visiting many shops and kiosks, picking up pins and other items which would quickly turn into sales. In the process, he touched countless items, brushed up against scores of people, and came into contact with germs that originated from every corner of the globe. He also came within breathing distance of hundreds of people. He touched many credit card machines, and Disneyland employees handled his credit card dozens of times.

Alex didn't even give any of this a second thought at the time. After seven hours or so in the park, he called it a day. With bags full of bounty, he exited satisfied, just as he had so many times before.

Several days passed, and he forgot all about his trip to Disney. He eased back into his routine of regular business activities. Approximately seventy-two hours after the trip to Disney, however, he began feeling…off. His throat began feeling sore. His body felt run-down.

The week that followed was a blur. He experienced constant body aches and dry coughs. Every time he closed his eyes to sleep he awoke a few minutes later, drenched in sweat. He couldn't stay asleep for more than thirty minutes at a time, and each time he awoke he had to change his clothes and bed sheets. He only slept a total of two hours per night for the duration of the seven-day sickness. He lost ten pounds, and it took a week to recover.

If the story ended there it would sound very bleak. But, though Alex tested positive for COVID-19, he didn't die. In fact, he didn't even have to go to the hospital. Sure, he felt quite sick for a week or so, but he made a full recovery within a few days. And in the months that followed, his ecommerce business began to thrive in ways he had never previously experienced. His sales multiplied. The pandemic, which forced so many aspects of our lives to go virtual, has greatly benefitted many Amazon sellers, as online sales have skyrocketed. Alex experienced this boom directly, even if he had to pivot with his supply methods.

What initially seemed like a crisis for Alex ended up becoming a catalyst for new success.

The pandemic, along with Alex's story, serve as the perfect illustration to set up the pages that follow. The pandemic has been billed as a scary, life-threatening, global threat. And while nearly 140 million people have been afflicted, just over 2% of those cases have resulted in death. I am not downplaying the severity of COVID-19 in any way, so please don't misunderstand me. What I am saying is that while it *can be* life-threatening, in *most* cases, it is not.

Likewise, while hundreds of sellers have come to me panicked about the need to write Plans of Action for Amazon, 98% of these clients have had successful appeals.

The parallels between Alex, the pandemic, POAs, and the purpose of this book should be coming into focus.

Currently there are over 1.6 million active, third-party sellers actively selling on the Amazon marketplace. While I don't have the exact numbers, the chances are great that nearly all of those sellers at some point in time are going to contract, or at least brush with, another type of sickness. The illness I refer to is *failing Amazon Account Health,* which results in Amazon requesting a POA.

There are specific reasons contracting "account disease" is so common among third-party sellers on the world's most popular marketplace. I will discuss these reasons in greater detail in the next chapter, but for now, the first thing to keep in mind (just like COVID-19) is there are both controllable and uncontrollable variables. Most sellers-whether due to negligence, ignorance, buyer complaints, competitors or shifts in Amazon policy-will find themselves needing to submit a POA in order to continue selling on Amazon.

If you have not yet been asked by Amazon to submit a POA in response to a performance notification, chances are good that you *will have to at some point.* By the end of these pages, I am confident you will be much better equipped to write your own POA. And while the request for a POA can be jarring and scary at first, what I am suggesting in this guide is that an appeal can actually become a catalyst for long-term growth for your company. In this sense, these pages are here to transform a common problem into a stimulus for hope, excitement, and success!

I attribute part of my success with appeals to the fact I have been an Amazon seller myself for over eight years. I have learned a great deal about Amazon through these years, and I hope you can benefit from my experience. Consider this guide both a resource for the immediate crisis and a reference for the bigger picture of your business goals.

In the pages that follow, we are going to discuss POAs from a holistic perspective. Together, we are going to win. However, while this guide serves as an introduction to basic principles and best practices, it is by no means exhaustive. While it will equip you with general advice for how to approach your appeal, it doesn't attempt to cover every specific situation. Even after implementing the tactics in this guide, you still might need support to tackle Account Health issues. This is where I should mention that I am available to help you personally, whether your needs are specific to a crisis or motivated by wanting to reach new goals. Please refer to the end of this guide and contact me immediately, if needed.

If you are currently dealing with an impending suspension or POA request, again, please do not panic. I recommend reading through these pages before you pick up the phone or send an email to Amazon. Through this process, you should become better equipped to think logically, rationally, and systematically. All of these are critical when it comes to winning appeals. I want you to feel confident that, after you have put the time into creating your own custom plan, you can submit it without fear of rejection.

Before you read any further, I have to urge you to avoid one common mistake: do not procrastinate with your response. Once they send you the initial request or notice, you are often up against a seventy-two hour clock to submit your plan. If you fail to do so, you could face the deactivation of your account. I don't want to see you lose your selling privileges because you feel ill-equipped, frustrated, or too overwhelmed to submit a POA. I also don't want you to fly blind into this situation, as that will most certainly lead to extended loss of your selling privileges.

You are going to get through this. You are not alone. In fact, what you are going through is extremely common. In the next chapter, you'll see some of the reasons why requests for Plans of Action are so common.

SCOTT MARGOLIUS

AMAZON PLANS OF ACTION

II. WHY PLANS OF ACTION ARE SO COMMON

Almost anyone, regardless of their stage in life, their background, or where they reside in the world, can start and run a successful ecommerce business. While selling on Amazon might not be the right business for everyone, Amazon offers seemingly limitless opportunities for thousands upon thousands of online merchants.

While selling on Amazon comes with the promise of great things, it is not a perfect system. New sellers can run into many landmines on the largest ecommerce platform in the world. I have witnessed businesses crumble when they are blindsided by Account Health problems.

You don't have to be one of these crumbling businesses, though. Grasping the key concepts in this guide will help you avoid major issues, or at least understand how to escape relatively unscathed from them.

Understanding why Amazon requests Plans of Action is the first step in writing a successful appeal. The customer experience, above all else, is the number one priority for Amazon. This philosophy, while great for customers, is the root of most requests for Plans of Action. They have built a reputation as a place where consumers can purchase items cheaper, faster, and with a no-questions-asked option to return anything for any reason. The customer is *always* right in the eyes of Amazon, even if they are wrong. As a consequence, third-party sellers are a lower priority than the customer. In light of this, there are three specific reasons POAs are so common, which I outline below.

First, Amazon is a guilty-until-proven-innocent system for sellers. So, if a customer complains, Amazon will hold *you* responsible, unless you are able to prove you were within policy on the transaction(s) in question. All complaints, violations, and negative feedback are immediately counted against the seller. Almost every single time there is a buyer complaint you must provide resolution steps because Amazon wants you to take responsibility, take action, and fix the problem(s).

Let's look at an example of how this plays out for the average seller. A client named Geoff had been selling on Amazon for about nine months. During that time, he had received a total of thirty-one seller feedback reviews. The first twenty-nine were five-stars, which meant his total feedback was 100%. However, after his initial run of positives, he received two negatives, making his feedback percentage 93%. He saw an immediate drop in sales, as his Buy Box win percentage dropped from 18% to 12%.

In looking into the negatives further, I was able to help him determine that both negatives were caused by customers who did not pay very close attention to the listing details. The listing in question was for a twenty-four-ounce bottle of shampoo, and the size of the bottle was clearly evident on the listing. The trouble came about because both buyers had previously purchased a thirty-six-ounce bottle. However, while they purchased from the same listing, it was a different variation on that listing. The buyers didn't realize the items they put in their carts were a different size from what they had previously purchased. This is a very common scenario, as many customers don't read listing details.

We worked together to communicate with the two buyers, and luckily, we received responses. The negative feedback took a week to resolve, at which point it was removed. Geoff's feedback score returned to 100%, and he returned to winning the Buy Box 18% of the time. For the ten days the negative feedback was on his account, however, his overall sales dropped by 30%.

This example wouldn't be very concerning if this was the end of the story. The negative feedback, however, caused a Performance Notification from Amazon Seller Performance which required a POA to appeal. The "case" (which appeared in Geoff's Account Health dashboard) was a negative mark for selling items that were "not as described." Any cases in your dashboard can affect your overall sales in a negative manner.

Due to circumstances mostly beyond his control, Geoff experienced a small taste of the ugly side of selling on Amazon-lost revenues and "dings" on his account which inched him closer to possible suspension. Customers didn't read the details of what they were buying from him. We worked together, submitted a plan, and potentially saved his business thousands of dollars in lost sales.

This brings me to my second reason why POAs are so common: Amazon wants sellers to be perfect. Not adequate, not above average, but *perfect*. Their system is engineered so the best sellers are featured on listings. It is a competition, essentially, where seller metrics play a huge role in determining who gets the sale. The algorithm Amazon uses to rank sellers consists of numerous variables, including feedback percentage, cancelled orders, valid tracking rate, returns, amount of feedback, time selling on the platform, Account Health, and more.

The point is, every single time you cancel an order, or a customer files an A-to-Z claim, or you receive even one instance of negative feedback, it counts against you. Between the many ways customers can complain, to the seemingly infinite ways to violate Amazon's policies, remaining perfect at all times is nearly impossible. Furthermore, the more violations, performance notifications, or negative Account Health metrics pile up, the more likely a request for a POA will become reality.

Finally, the third reason why Plans of Action are so common is simply this: Amazon policy. As I mentioned, it can be immensely challenging to remain completely compliant with the rules at all times. There are many intricate policies and they are constantly changing. New policies are being added on a regular basis. When you realize the amount of traffic, transactions, buyers, and genuinely shady practices Amazon has to police, it's not difficult to understand why. There are so many rules in place for a reason, and many of them were implemented in response to scams, legal issues, legislation, and customer issues they have faced in the past. It can require full-time effort from at least one dedicated employee on your team to truly maintain constant, complete compliance.

For example, Albert, a seller located in southern California, was heavily dependent on one manufacturer for sourcing. This source represented roughly 80% of Albert's revenue. Then, due to COVID-19, the factory closed. Albert was left desperate and scrambling for fresh inventory because his Amazon business was his only income. He began sourcing well-ranked ASINs in the household category (which were largely out of stock on Amazon). In a different context, he may have been onto a winning strategy. But in this case, he was sourcing cleaning products and other items considered household essentials.

He found immediate success, as there was very little competition on these listings. He sold out of most of these products daily and he was able to charge three to four times his cost. But, Albert was in violation of Amazon's Fair Pricing policies:
https://sellercentral.amazon.com/gp/help/external/G5TUVJKZHUVMN77V.

After three weeks of great sales, he received five policy violations and was asked to submit a POA or face suspension.

I wrote a POA for him which was accepted, but that is not the point. Amazon does not allow you to price items more than ten percent above market prices across the web. If you do this regularly (especially in riskier categories), sooner or later you may be facing a suspension. Albert was just doing business as usual in an attempt to survive. He had no malicious intent. And yet, he was in violation of Amazon policy.

At any point in time, you can be flagged for violating a policy you may not even be aware of. It should be noted that these Fair Pricing policies were rarely enforced prior to this, except for situations involving natural disasters.

Think about this in terms of driving a car. You can almost always get away with driving five MPH over the speed limit without a problem...until the police decide they want to pull you over. The fact is, Amazon's approach to their own rules is always in flux, and you never really know when they are going to crack down.

So, let's take a step back and evaluate all of this information. As a seller, remember, you are "guilty until proven innocent." You also have to constantly monitor pricing, as well as keep up with ever-changing policies. Plus, you frequently have to deal with shady or demanding customers. Can you see why nearly every seller will face the need to submit a POA at some point? It really is inevitable, unless you are one of a very small minority.

The fact is, if you are going to have long-term success, you must learn how to successfully appeal violations. The sooner you accept this, the sooner you can get to the place you always dreamed of-sustainable, repeatable, consistent, reliable profits. I have witnessed many sellers who gave up in frustration before they reached their goals. Don't be one of the many who fold too early. There is still plenty of hope for you and your business, if you stick with me!

AMAZON PLANS OF ACTION

AMAZON PLANS OF ACTION

III. WHAT IS A PLAN OF ACTION?

I have found in my years of helping sellers write Plans of Action that there is some confusion regarding what Amazon is actually requesting of you. Before we can begin strategizing how to approach your POA, it is important to address some common misconceptions in order to then establish a working definition. In other words, we have to understand what a POA is *not* in order to establish what a POA *is*. This will lay the proper foundation for an approach which will give you the best chance of winning your appeal.

Just to be clear: A POA is *not a legal defense to Amazon, an admission of guilt, or just an apology*. If you approach your plan from any of these standpoints, you are more likely to lose your appeal. A successful POA involves a simple communication of understanding what went wrong, then a clear statement of the actions which you have taken to correct the problem.

A PLAN OF ACTION IS NOT YOUR LEGAL DEFENSE TO AMAZON

Jim's Amazon business was clearing $20,000.00 in profit every month. He had a staff of three full-time employees, and was experiencing significant growth. Within a couple weeks, several violations hit his account. These were due to mistakes he made with inventory prep. Incorrect units were shipped to FBA, and customer complaints led to the threat of suspension, pending a POA submission.

To Jim, it was insulting that Amazon had asked him to appeal in order to retain his selling privileges. He had invested an enormous amount of energy into developing his business, and was doing all the right things. He paid attention to every detail. Jim had approached all aspects of his infrastructure with the utmost professionalism.

He truly felt that Amazon had no *right* to threaten his business.

Prior to calling me, he sent a very frustrated response to Amazon Seller Support, then contacted an attorney. He was contemplating arbitration, but contacted me just prior to pursuing legal action.

After about an hour on the phone, I was able to calm him down. I explained that Amazon is not "out to get him" or his business. I reminded him that Amazon doesn't usually issue these types of requests because of anything personal, or even *legal* in nature. I assured him that Amazon is basically a machine that crunches numbers and spits out data. I advised him to respond in a calm, rational manner with the details they needed to keep his account active. Finally, I shared that nearly every single one of my clients who took a non-combative posture with their appeal eventually won.

All Amazon wanted Jim to demonstrate was that he understood the problem, and that he was going to do whatever was necessary to avoid the same problem in the future. He just needed to communicate this without any defensiveness.

It really *is* that simple.

No matter how much you want to stick up for yourself in your POA, you will not get the desired result if you do so. Amazon is not a court of law. You are selling on *their* platform. They hold *all* the cards. Attempting to prove that the customer was wrong, that your supplier was wrong, or that *they* are wrong is usually the opposite of what Amazon is looking for from you.

I can't stress this enough.

You are a guest in their home. You either play by their rules, or they will show you the door. That may sound cold, but it is a fact. You don't have *rights*, per se. Even with the recently revised Seller Agreement, Amazon isn't a democracy. We must accept this if we want to sell on their platform.

As any polite house guest should, when you violate the rules of the house, your only real defense is to humbly take responsibility for what has happened and change your behavior. This is the professional response, given the reality of the situation.

I worked with Jim through several rounds of editing, and we formulated a POA that was polite, succinct, and devoid of any defensive language. When he finally accepted the fact that Amazon is not a court of law, and that we weren't mounting a defense of his "rights," it was smooth sailing. His account was cleared within a week of his POA submission, and he continues to make great profits to this day.

A PLAN OF ACTION IS NOT AN ADMISSION OF GUILT

Brenda knew she had been riding a fine line. In order to grow her business, she had been sourcing inventory from Target through a major liquidator. She found a deal on two pallets of beauty items that would allow her to generate a 150% ROI. The only problem was that the liquidation items she purchased were customer returns. In other words, many of the items she was obtaining were not considered "New" by Amazon standards. Here is a link to Amazon's definition of "New." Every seller should be familiar with the Condition Guidelines, part of the TOS or Terms of Service: **https://sellercentral.amazon.com/gp/help/external/200339950.** Another great place for sellers to learn about the rules and best practices Amazon recommends is in Seller University: **https://sellercentral.amazon.com/learn/.**

Since Brenda had been struggling for months to meet her personal sales goals in order to stay above water, this opportunity seemed timely. Though she knew the condition of the items could possibly cause problems, her desperation for profits made the risk seem worthwhile. In the end, the risk was definitely *not* worth it (and almost NEVER is, if that risk is associated with item condition issues).

She shipped 50% of her "new" inventory into FBA, doing her best to clean up as much of the used product as she could. When I say "clean up," I mean *condition hacking.* There is training on the web about how to do this, especially for certain categories, such as books. My recommendation is to tread lightly, because this practice can get you into big trouble with Amazon. In this case, Brenda knew some of the items she was shipping in might trigger customer complaints, but again, she was desperate. She held the other half of her "new" inventory back for merchant fulfillment.

Sure enough, after a short period of time, the issues ensued. First, a counterfeit complaint came from an upset buyer who asserted that because the original packaging had been removed (the item in question was mascara), it was not authentic. Several additional condition complaints followed, with buyers stating they received used products. She was hit with several IP violations, as well. These violations snowballed, and she soon found herself in the all-too-familiar situation of having to submit a Plan of Action in order to continue selling.

Brenda came to me in a pretty sad state. She felt guilty for trying to cheat the system, but she also admitted she made the decision out of desperation. She said, "If it wasn't so hard to scale my business, I wouldn't have taken these shortcuts."

When she first contacted me, she had already written a POA and was asking for help with her final edit. In the draft, she did not give specific details as to what she was going to do to fix the problems. Worse yet, her invoice was not helpful at all since it wasn't manifested.

This is an all-too-common situation. Many times, when sellers receive the POA request from Seller Performance, they act as though they have been caught in a crime. In response, they assume a confession will assuage the authorities, much like a plea bargain. Again, Amazon is not the government!

You *do* need to take responsibility for mistakes which occur in your account, but you do not need to paint yourself in a bad light. Seller Performance isn't looking for a conviction. They simply want to know that you understand the cause of the situation, that you have made yourself familiar with their policies, and that you have implemented practical steps to ensure future compliance.

If you treat your POA like an admission of guilt, hoping it will reduce or remove your sentence, you are missing the point entirely. You need to take responsibility for the problem, but you do not need to take the posture of a criminal. You haven't been caught committing a crime.

Remain focused on the facts of what happened and why. Then explain the specific steps you are implementing to ensure the mistakes don't happen again. This simple approach will give you the best chance of winning your appeal, and this approach got Brenda over the finish line.

A PLAN OF ACTION IS NOT JUST AN APOLOGY

Mike had been running ragged since sales picked up on Black Friday, and he could hardly keep up with the orders that had come flooding in. He went from selling $300.00 gross per day to more than $1,500.00. He was not accustomed to that sales volume, and did not have the processes in place to stay organized. For six weeks straight, he was working fourteen-hour days. Inevitably, details began to slip, and mistakes were made. He had enough late orders that Amazon suspended his account.

Mike came to me with a prewritten Plan of Action in-hand. While very sincere, I knew, after reading it, that he would not be reinstated if we didn't make adjustments. In his initial draft, he took responsibility for his mistakes, citing the fact that he was unprepared for the significant increase in sales. He expressed deep regret over violating Amazon's policy, along with how much he understood the value of the customer experience. All of these things are great to mention, but Amazon is looking for more than an apology. They are also looking for measurable and verifiable pivots in your business. You have to give them *the right information* so they can feel confident that you've addressed the situation thoroughly.

Remember, Amazon is not a person, or even a group of people. "It" doesn't have feelings. This might come as a shock to you, but you are one of millions of sellers. You are just a number. A tiny cog. You don't have a relationship with Amazon, no matter how big you are. They have little vested interest in your individual success. While you provide them income as part of the third-party seller ecosystem, their larger concern is in protecting their brand and customer experience. So, your POA is not going to appeal to Amazon's conscience. Amazon has no conscience. They aren't holding a grudge. They are not angry. They are not targeting you.

These statements may sound cold, but there is actually comfort in all of this. All they want to know is that you are a professional seller who will make the necessary changes to adhere to their policies. Period. End of Story.

After sharing with Mike what Seller Performance needed from him, we used the first part of his POA. Then, we added specifics about hiring employees, his employee handbook, new third-party software, and changes to how he monitored his account health dashboard. We also demonstrated that he had become significantly more educated about Amazon policy.

His selling privileges were reinstated two weeks later.

AMAZON PLANS OF ACTION

COMMON MISTAKES WHEN WRITING PLANS OF ACTION

Before I define, in simple terms, what a Plan of Action actually is, I want to address three common mistakes sellers typically make when they write their plans themselves.

1. *Overinflated language.* In nearly every POA I receive from clients, there is an abundance of flowery language. Amazon isn't looking for fluff because it confuses the message you should be sending. In some situations, excess fluff can also communicate a lack of sincerity. This is not unlike high school English class. Since the dawn of time, students have tried to pull the wool over the eyes of their teachers by using big words and repeated phrases in their essays. And just like English class, the teacher is never fooled. The same principle rings true with Seller Performance. You should keep things as simple as possible. Otherwise, the meat of your message could become convoluted. Seller Performance representatives are taught to base their decision on the bottom line of what is being communicated. They will not approve your appeal if your communication is more fluff than fact.

2. *Not Specific Enough.* Nearly every time a POA is rejected, it is because Amazon demands more specifics from the seller. Most often they either require a clearer root cause or more detailed corrective actions. You have to *clearly* demonstrate that you know the cause of the problem(s) and are making *specific* changes in your business to comply with Amazon policy. There is a big difference between stating, "I adjusted prices in my inventory," and, "We applied the Competitive External Price rule to every single ASIN in our inventory, and will utilize the pricing automation function in the seller dashboard for all inventory items in the future." Make sure to refer to your suppliers by name, employees by their title, and reference specific Amazon policies wherever possible. If you make a change to your infrastructure, you have to tell them specifically what you did. If you added processes to your daily routine in order to combat the problem Seller Performance is addressing, explain it in detail, but also as succinctly as possible. Be pointed, brief, and don't mention anything irrelevant.

3. *Improper Tone.* I already mentioned this, but it bears repeating because it is very important. I can't tell you how many times I have received an initial POA from a client with a combative tone. You cannot even hint to Seller Performance that you are anything but thankful for the opportunity to continue selling on *their* platform. You cannot in any way blame customers, even if some of the blame actually *does* fall on them. You cannot make excuses, and you cannot cite

the Amazon system as a cause. The tone of your appeal must convey humility.

WHAT A PLAN OF ACTION ACTUALLY *IS*

A successful Plan of Action is not complicated. In fact, most of the POAs I write are two pages or less. A properly written plan communicates clear facts in a simple manner and gives specific details. A good POA works within an outline which clearly demonstrates your understanding of what happened and why. Then, it shows the changes you have implemented, as well as what you have done to prevent the same thing from ever happening again.

The whole point of your plan is to make certain that Amazon understands you are willing to do anything and everything necessary to comply with their rules. You also must communicate that your priorities are the same as theirs. Remember, Amazon is not interested in your feelings. They are not interested in your excuses. They are not convicting you of a crime and they are not targeting you. Amazon also is not interested in your profits (or lack thereof). At the end of the day, Amazon cares most about protecting the customer experience. This is why their policies are in place. Therefore, all communication, language, and tone must support the fact that you are going to align every detail of your business to said policies.

There you have it! Now that you have a better understanding of what a POA actually is, we'll dive into the actual process...one that involves much more than writing!

AMAZON PLANS OF ACTION

IV. FOUNDATIONAL RESEARCH: DETECTIVE WORK AS THE FIRST STEP TO WINNING YOUR APPEAL

Alan awoke with a sharp pain in his lower, left abdomen. It was a pain he had never felt before. After doing some research online, he came to the conclusion that the cause of his pain was most likely a hernia. Although he could not remember any activities that could have caused this, he proceeded with his day as if this diagnosis was fact. One week later, the pain had not abated. So, he went to see his family physician.

After conducting an examination, the doctor offered a different conclusion completely. He was almost certain that Alan was not suffering from a hernia, but diverticulitis (an inflammation of the lower intestine). To confirm the diagnosis, he suggested that Alan adopt a liquid diet for several days. Sure enough, after about seventy-two hours had passed, the pain subsided.

He revisited the doctor, who helped Alan develop a new nutrition plan. This involved abstaining from gluten and dairy, as well as increasing his fiber intake. Months have passed since the initial inflammation, and he has not dealt with any abdominal pain. He has stuck closely to his diet recommendations, and as long as he does, he should not have much trouble in the foreseeable future.

What would have happened had Alan not taken the steps necessary to find the actual cause of his pain? Most likely his issues would have progressed until he faced hospitalization or worse.

AMAZON PLANS OF ACTION

The point, as it relates to our discussion of Plans of Action, is that when problems arise you must determine the exact source of the issue in order to treat it. It requires detective work, and you must be willing to do whatever is necessary to determine the root cause. The prognosis (as well as the treatment) of the situation is entirely dependent upon your research. You simply cannot know why you are being flagged by Amazon to submit a Plan of Action until you do all the work necessary to uncover the *why*. And you certainly cannot skip this step before attempting to write your POA. Doing so will greatly decrease your chances of success.

Here's an example of this process, from a recent client:

Mark was in shock. He could not, for the life of him, figure out why his seller account was in a review status. While he had received some marks against his Account Health over the previous six months, those incidents were scattered across many months, as well as different categories of violations. He had two IP complaints, three product condition complaints, one listing policy violation, two restricted product policy violations, and two product safety complaints. He hadn't appealed these violations, as he thought he rectified them by simply removing these products from his inventory and deleting the listings.

When I asked him about what happened with these violations, he really didn't have answers. He had never looked into the actual cases because he just assumed they would melt off his Account Health dashboard, since he deleted the listings. Unfortunately, Mark did not understand that each of these violations had a cumulative, negative effect on his standing with Amazon.

In order to help Mark resolve all this, he and I had to execute perhaps the most important step in submitting a successful POA: determining the reasons why the violations had occurred. To put it more precisely, we had to determine why Amazon *thought* he was in violation of their policies. We had to get inside of Amazon's head, so to speak.

We made a spreadsheet, and spent a solid five hours investigating. We scoured every aspect of his account, leaving no stone unturned. We gained the insight necessary to submit his POA, and it was eventually accepted. Had we not done the research to determine the causes, we would have been flying blind with his plan, and his chances of winning his appeal would have been greatly reduced. We'll cover the areas which need to be investigated in the next chapter.

The research you perform to uncover the sources of your problems will dictate the strategy of your entire appeal. Amazon expects you to know their policies, and holds you responsible for any and all violations. They don't always give you straight answers or information on why cases occur, or why they want you to submit an appeal. In fact, more often than not, you will not have all the information you need to submit a winning appeal simply by reading the performance notification or email they send you. So, you need to become an investigator. This requires you to employ the same tactics any real detective would utilize in order to solve a crime. You need to learn to see the case(s) before you from the perspective of all parties involved. Most of all, you must learn to *think* like the Amazon Seller Performance Team.

When a crime scene investigator does their work, they take the facts for what they are. They don't read into them, or overthink. They let the evidence speak for itself before trying to connect all of the pieces. You must do the same. The more objective and dispassionate you can be, the stronger your POA will be. If you jump to conclusions prematurely, you may find yourself on the wrong path. You have to piece the data together and make sense of it. Again, the more you can process the data through the lens of Amazon's viewpoint, the better your chances.

Most violations have hints to causation buried deep in your account, and it is your job to uncover them. We are going to walk through the most common places to find clues in the paragraphs that follow, keeping in mind the vast majority of Account Health issues have to do with customer complaints. Each of the following sections explores a specific area of your account you must scour for clues.

PERFORMANCE NOTIFICATIONS

When you have an issue with your Account Health, Amazon will usually notify you of it via email and/or Performance Notifications in your seller dashboard. I say "usually," because Amazon isn't always consistent or predictable with their communication. Sometimes you will get an email. Sometimes you will see a case in your Account Health dashboard. Sometimes you will only receive a Performance Notification. You could receive any of the above many months after the initial violation or issue occurred, or within twenty four hours of the event.

It is important to note that regardless of how Amazon notifies you, you must *take action* when they do. After calming your emotions, your digging should begin immediately. I should also remind you of the fact that you should *never* respond to Amazon's communication with *anything* except for what they are asking for. What many sellers don't realize is that when you respond to a request for a Plan of Action with questions or any other type of communication besides a well thought-out plan, Amazon actually counts it as an appeal attempt. They treat *any* communication (no matter how brief or pointed) as an official POA. So, if you are responding with anything *but* a POA, you are giving them something they do not want. You cannot respond with a request for clarification, a question, or even a simple statement. Seller Performance will almost always respond with a request for more information, which will cause your inquiry to count as a failed appeal attempt.

The very first thing to do, in terms of research, is to read (then reread) Amazon's communication with you. Sometimes they provide only one or two sentences that communicate anything insightful. For example, the policies referenced may sometimes be your only clues as to what they are thinking. In cases where the communication doesn't provide any clarity, you cannot reply with a question. There are other ways to decode what is truly happening, which I will discuss shortly.

Sometimes Amazon will suggest a call to speak to a member of the Account Health team, and in certain instances, they will even call *you*. Make sure you don't miss the opportunity to speak with them if they attempt to contact you. In fact, this is preferable to calling *them*, because the rep who is reaching out to you will already be acquainted with your case. During the call, remember you are still in detective mode! Ask as many relevant questions as possible. Remember, your attitude on the call is important. Don't ever be defensive or give them additional reasons to flag your account. Be courteous and don't give away any unnecessary information. I always advise clients to write out their questions in advance because sticking to a script eliminates the possibility for error. If you initiated the call instead of them, keep in mind you can always call back and you may get a rep who is more helpful or knowledgeable. This can take several attempts. Make sure you block out plenty of time for the call, without interruptions.

Unless you are in outright violation of Amazon policy, a buyer complaint/return most likely drove Amazon to take action against you. You must understand that the return process for customers is very flawed, and in many ways, stacked against the seller. Buyers must choose from a list of return reason categories, and because these categories are so broad, they may not wholly apply to their specific situation. This makes your detective work all the more vital.

Let me give you an example of how this can play out. Not long ago, Jason came to me with a complaint he received for inauthentic products. "Inauthenticity" can be a very vague term in the Amazon world and it is associated with an inordinate number of buyer complaints. Customers are actually *incentivized* to choose "inauthentic" as the reason for a return. When they choose this reason, they receive free return shipping (while other choices in the return menu don't necessarily offer this).

After checking the listing in question thoroughly, we discovered the inventory Jason sent into FBA was the previous year's version of the item. However, the product photo on the listing was a depiction of the newest version. Everything else was exactly the same. The packaging was the only difference. Amazon wasn't actually accusing Jason of having inauthentic products. Again, there was simply no other option for the buyer to qualify for free return shipping and a refund. Besides choosing "Not as Described," there probably wasn't another relevant category for the buyer to select. It is important to note that your inventory must match listings perfectly, otherwise buyers will eventually complain, which will put your account at risk.

Amazon makes it very difficult for the buyer to find remedies when they receive something that isn't *exactly* what they thought they were purchasing. So, the return process itself actually *pushes* buyers toward making false accusations against sellers. Unfortunately, this has been a broken part of the Amazon system for years. The sooner you accept this as part of the game, the better off you will be.

Notice I use the word "sometimes" frequently. This is because there aren't hard and fast rules to Amazon's "behavior" in terms of Performance Notifications. Every situation is unique, just as every seller account is unique. This makes your work as a CSI agent all the more important. There are almost always clues, but it is up to you to uncover them.

REFUNDS AND RETURNS

Refunds and returns are where you will often find the most telling information for your Plan of Action. To access this information, visit the Manage Orders section of your seller dashboard. On the Manage Orders page, there's a search field on the upper right. Select "ASIN" in the drop-down menu, then enter the ASIN number for which you are searching. You will want to repeat this process for each ASIN which needs appealing. You must identify all orders of the ASIN in question, focusing on the month prior to the notification/case/complaint which led to the request for the POA.

Any returns or refunds will be highlighted in red as you scroll through your sold transactions. Click on each one and look at the transactions carefully, noting any comments or feedback associated with the returned/refunded items. If a buyer was frustrated enough to communicate with Amazon regarding the transaction, they typically leave some sort of comment. This area of your account can contain similar information as the sections I mention below. Note that the "Manage Orders" section can be a more comprehensive area to search because it will also show MFN orders.

FBA RETURNS REPORTS

"FBA Returns Reports" is another section of your account for discovery, where you may find some interesting data which could shed light on your situation. To access this area, select "Reports" from the top of the screen in Seller Central. Hover over the drop-down menu and choose "Fulfillment." Look at the menu on the left where you will find "Customer Concessions." Select "FBA Customer Returns." Enter the ASIN(s) from your case(s), and choose "Last 30 Days" for your filter criteria. Scour the report for reasons items were returned. You should see hyperlinks for return reasons. If you click these, you should see some clues. Often, the information found from this returns area holds the key to unlocking the root cause you need for your POA.

FEEDBACK

You can find "Feedback" under the "Performance" menu in your seller dashboard, in the drop-down. Look for any feedback which is associated with the ASIN(s) connected to your case. Research the thirty days prior to the complaint(s), looking for any negative comments or keywords. This is pretty self-explanatory, and doesn't require much digging. If a buyer says something less than positive, it will be very apparent.

MESSAGES

Sometimes buyers will use buyer/seller messaging to contact you directly when they are dissatisfied with some aspect of a transaction. While dealing with messaging can sometimes seem like a pain, communication from buyers can actually be very helpful in regards to your detective work. When buyers contact you directly (instead of reaching out to Amazon first), that is your opportunity to take care of them, resolve the situation immediately, and prevent recourse from Amazon. If the buyer is indicating any kind of dissatisfaction and provides their reasons, you can fix things for them on the spot, and it will prevent further issues later. Messaging usually provides insight into what the buyer is thinking. This can make figuring out what to address in your Plan of Action much easier. So, start by going through your messages one by one. Usually, you won't need to go back more than thirty days from the time you receive the notice to determine if any of the key ASIN(s) are referenced.

PRODUCT REVIEWS

The "Product Reviews" section can give clues to overall consumer attitudes. Chances are, if there are problems with an ASIN in terms of product condition, manufacturer defects, or other quality-related issues, you won't be the only seller affected by those product issues. Sometimes you will even receive an ASIN violation associated with a*nother seller's inventory*! Yes, you read that correctly. While it's rare, it definitely happens.

In order to read product eviews, you have to visit the main Amazon website or use the Amazon app. You cannot do this from the seller dashboard or the seller app. So, visit Amazon.com and enter the referenced ASIN(s) as you would if you were shopping. Clicking on the review number next to the stars should take you to the customer reviews page. If you click on the reviews under the summary of all ratings, a new screen will pop up where you can filter product reviews by "All Critical" as well as "Most Recent." Look for negative comments from all buyers and any patterns of complaints which could apply to your situation. Complaints, even if they are not in reference to specific orders from your customers, can give you clues as to what may be happening with your inventory.

VOICE OF THE CUSTOMER

In Seller Central, under the Performance drop-down, you will see an option to choose "Voice of the Customer." You should spend some time investigating this area, and pay attention to any items that aren't marked in green. This is a good summary section that will help you stay on top of issues and also prevent future problems. You will learn of concerns Amazon has with your inventory. The information in this section could be relevant to what you'll address in your Plan of Action, depending on your findings.

REVIEWS ON OTHER PLATFORMS

As a last resort, it can sometimes be helpful to search for product reviews on other platforms and websites. Target, eBay, Walmart, and Google searches are the best places to start, and you can typically find a good deal of information about consumer attitudes toward a given product by spending five minutes doing this. This is definitely not the first place to look, but your efforts here can produce surprising results in certain instances.

For example, a client came to me with a very confusing situation regarding a complaint about a particular model of shoe he had been selling. He sourced directly with the manufacturer. His inventory was flawless, and he had a very well-developed prep/inspection infrastructure for his business. He knew the items were in pristine condition. The sizes were correct. Everything seemed to be in order, as it was a product he had been selling for a very long time. But, out of the blue, the ASIN was flagged, and he was asked to appeal to continue selling this product.

After searching all of the places mentioned previously, the results were inconclusive. At this point, we conducted a Google search. After doing some digging, we discovered there had been recent changes in the manufacturing process for this particular shoe model. While the materials, colors, look, and design were the same, the shoes were being manufactured in a different factory. The result was a shoe that felt different to the customer. The fit of the actual product had changed enough to trigger buyer dissatisfaction. We would not have discovered this without a Google search. His entire Plan of Action was shaped around this information, and the ASIN was reinstated shortly thereafter.

CHAPTER IV. CONCLUSIONS: WHAT TO DO WITH YOUR DISCOVERIES

The data you uncover will be a function of how much time and effort you invest in your detective work. There are many instances where the steps I have outlined in this chapter have led to definitive answers. But, this is not always the case. There are certain instances where you cannot determine with any degree of certainty why you have been flagged. In cases like this, your detective work has not been in vain. Even if you do not find obvious answers, you *will* find clues as to what is *probably* going on.

When no clear causation is revealed through research, my plan is always to craft a Plan of Action which addresses the *most likely* cause(s) of the issue(s). When you write this type of appeal, it is usually enough to win, so long as you are specific about what you have done to correct all related issues in your account.

Remember, a big part of your POA is about communicating to Amazon that you understand and take responsibility for the root cause of the problem. Your research lays the foundation for success. If you have been thorough, you will be in great shape. A winning appeal is not far away!

AMAZON PLANS OF ACTION

V. FINAL CONSIDERATIONS BEFORE WRITING

ACTION BEFORE WORDS

By this point you are probably thinking, *when are we going to start writing?!* Hopefully it's apparent now why I recommend proper preparation before the actual composition of your Plan of Action. Writing is the last step if you want to be successful. There is no way around this fact. Don't skip or gloss over the steps I have already outlined. They may actually save your business!

This whole process is actually about both *becoming* and *demonstrating* that you are now running a policy-compliant operation. You must actually do the things you say you've done and are going to do; simply telling them what you think they want to hear is a losing proposition. You can't make empty promises in an attempt to fool Seller Performance. Amazon will see through it if this is your approach, so your only real option is to *really make the necessary changes*.

Let's revisit a previous example from an earlier chapter to help illustrate the need for real-life changes to your business in connection with your POA. To refresh, a client was facing a suspension for price gouging. When COVID-19 hit, he was unable to source products from his most significant supplier. To compensate, he began sourcing household essentials products. Since he was the only seller on many of these listings, he was able to raise his prices and charge double (and even triple) the typical, pre-pandemic prices. But then, he was hit with multiple violations, and Seller Performance demanded a POA.

AMAZON PLANS OF ACTION

The majority of our efforts for this plan were focused on demonstrating to Amazon the specific actions taken to ensure no pricing violations would ever occur again. These actions included the following:

1. We held an immediate, emergency, all-staff meeting to read through Amazon's specific policies regarding pricing, price gouging, and the Competitive External Price rule. This meeting included thorough study of all articles released in the Help section since the start of the pandemic.

2. We revised the employee handbook to include specific training related to all Amazon pricing policies addressed in the meeting. This ensured all future employees will be educated upon hiring.

3. We assigned Bill Alice, our bookkeeper, to monitor pricing on a daily basis. He researches competitive pricing across all inventory, not only on Amazon, but also across the web.

4. We deleted all affected ASINs, all similar ASINs, and removed all affected inventory from both MFN and FBA. We removed all household essential items from our inventory, and will never overprice items in this category again.

5. Bill Alice reconfigured the settings for all inventory in our third-party repricing software. He set all minimum and maximum pricing on all inventory according to the Competitive External Price rule.

6. We have made certain, after checking Google, Target, Walmart, and eBay, that no prices were more than ten percent above the average market price, or MAP. Also, we established fail-safes in place via repricing software to ensure prices would never climb above this metric.

As you can see, these were very specific (and even drastic) measures. In this POA, he pledged to completely change how he approached sourcing, listing, and managing his inventory. Through the process, he made a decision: he was willing to do anything and everything necessary to be compliant, and in turn, remain a long-term seller on Amazon.

The most important thing to note was that he implemented all of this *prior to writing his POA*. You must be willing to do the same. You must make specific, provable changes that Amazon can readily verify in your account. If you say you deleted all of your inventory, your account must show that you have already done it. If you missed deleting (or adjusting) just one listing upon submitting your POA, that could be enough to result in rejection. Don't miss the point here: if you actually apply your changes, it is almost guaranteed to prevent the same problems from surfacing again. Unfortunately, if you land on the radar of Seller Performance a second time, they will not be as forgiving.

Be willing to go the extra mile and cover every base possible, even if you are "innocent" of policy violations. Use the request for a POA as an opportunity to fortify and improve your business. Familiarize yourself with Amazon policies, as they change constantly. You have to demonstrate to Seller Performance that you run a professional business, and you take your selling privileges seriously.

Action is Amazon's love language for POAs. That is why they use the word itself for the description of this process!

THE LANGUAGE OF PLANS OF ACTION

Seller Performance reps are trained to look for and understand the bottom line of your communication. Anything beyond simple, factual language runs the risk of missing the mark, thus jeopardizing your appeal. For example, I recently saw a Plan of Action rejected because the Account Health representative said the plan was "too college." She explained that all the necessary information was there, but the language used was too complicated. This perfectly illustrates the point I am trying to make!

Another thing to note: Seller Performance reps are held to very strict standards. Many of the policies and headaches you deal with as a seller are actually the result of previous scams (and the subsequent policy/enforcement reactions have been necessary on Amazon's part). Reps face consequences from their superiors if they approve an appeal for a seller who continues to violate policy after submitting a POA. These employees must process a certain number of cases per day, or their jobs are on the line. They have very little time to weed out the scammers from the legitimate business owners, so you must convey that you are the latter with everything you say and do.

The language of POAs is a basic one. Be concise and don't give Seller Performance any reason to be distracted by superfluous language or content!

OTHER SUGGESTIONS BEFORE WRITING

Before writing, you should close the listing(s) in question, rather than delete it (them). The reason for this is that you can still edit the listing when you close it, and updating can sometimes be the key to fixing the issue.

You should make certain you have resolved any customer issues before submitting your Plan of Action. This may include responding to messages and/or resolving any disputes. This may also include processing any returns or refunds. In your plan, you should briefly explain all of the customer service resolution steps you have taken.

A final thought before we write, and this is important: *there is no specific template for a successful POA*. I have witnessed many failed attempts to "reuse" successful plans. As I have said, every situation is unique, and while your situation may seem straight-forward, you may not have the full picture of what the Seller Performance reps are seeing in your account. In addition, you should assume that Amazon uses software to curtail plagiarism. The point is, don't copy someone else's homework! If you use a cookie-cutter format, you'll most likely get a form letter rejection in response. Your POA should be personalized and unique to your situation and *in your own voice*.

It should be noted, again, that I rarely submit a plan that is longer than two pages. If you write clearly, succinctly, and without filler, you should not need more space to address the problems.

Now, it's really time. Your chances of winning your appeal are connected to your commitment to this process, so if you have skimped on any part, now would be the time to revisit the previous pages. If you have applied everything thus far, you can feel confident moving forward to the actual writing process.

AMA

AMAZON PLANS OF ACTION

VI. IT'S FINALLY TIME...TO WRITE

You have made a decision to stick it out and do whatever is necessary to move forward as a seller. You have caught your breath, worked your way through your initial emotions, and thwarted all airs of defensiveness. You have completed the detective work to determine the cause of the complaints, and the reasons behind the request for a Plan of Action. You have identified the changes which need to be made, and you have actually done the work to implement them.

Congratulations! You are now *ready* to write your POA.

There are five distinct parts to a POA (six, if you include any additional information). They include:

1. INTRODUCTION

2. ROOT CAUSE

3. STEPS YOU HAVE TAKEN TO RESOLVE THE ISSUE

4. STEPS YOU HAVE TAKEN TO PREVENT FUTURE ISSUES

5. CONCLUSION.

Each part is connected to the others, but is wholly independent as well. I will cover each of these sections in turn, keeping things as straight-forward as I can, with examples. I will contrast what I would consider a good example with a poor one for each section. I have chosen to use examples which are specifically

AMAZON PLANS OF ACTION

related to Amazon's Covid-19 crackdown on pricing policy.

I cannot overemphasize the fact that if you choose to copy/apply someone else's successful POA to your own situation, you are doing so at your own risk. And yet, despite the fact that I am emphasizing this in back-to-back sections of the book, I am certain that there will be some who copy and paste the examples I am about to provide into their own plans. Language that once worked for someone else will stop working. You want to use plain terms that apply to you and your specific situation. The "word soup" approach (using a collection of statements that are lifted from other successful POAs) will fall on deaf ears.

Let's move on to looking at the specific sections needed in every POA.

INTRODUCTION

I suggest a one-to-two sentence introduction to Seller Performance to set the tone of your Plan of Action. It should convey a general summary statement about what the document is communicating overall. Essentially, you should thank them for the opportunity to address the situation, mention why you were notified, and include your reason for writing the plan.

GOOD EXAMPLE:

"Dear Seller Performance,

Thank you for giving us the opportunity to address your concerns regarding asin B07XYZ89. We were made aware that we have violated Amazon's Fair Pricing policies. We apologize for the issues we've caused and we will do anything necessary to make certain we never violate Amazon pricing policy for any reason."

POOR EXAMPLE:

"Dear Seller Performance,

We received notification that we need to submit a Plan of Action in order to continue selling on Amazon. To our knowledge, we have not violated any policies, and would like to bring to your attention several customer complaints which were no fault of our own, which caused this unjust scenario for us."

A good introduction is contrite and thankful. It conveys a willingness to comply and do whatever is necessary to make Amazon happy. The poor one is defensive and frustrated, and if sent through, the Seller Performance representative who reads it will almost certainly deny the POA before reading further. Any language which conveys even a hint of defensiveness could cause your POA to be denied.

If you keep your introduction simple and direct (while specifically referencing the issue at hand with a humble attitude) you should be on the right track.

Let's move on...

THE ROOT CAUSE

After your humble and gracious introduction, you have to lay out the root causes of the issue(s). This is the foundation of your Plan of Action, and it is the reason you spent so much effort on researching the problems. Without the research, you wouldn't be able to pinpoint what is truly going on, because (as you now should know) many times Amazon isn't going to tell you the root cause of the issue. If you have done the digging, you should have a clear picture in mind of the root cause, or at the very least a *sound theory* on what Amazon thinks is happening.

Again, the most important thing to note here is that you have to get inside the brain of the teacher, so to speak. You have to give Amazon reason(s) to believe *you understand the problem from their perspective*. You have to clearly identify the mistakes you made which resulted in the violation(s) or customer complaints. Then, you have to explain how you resolved those problems.

Remember, it doesn't matter if you disagree with Amazon or the customer. It doesn't matter how unjust or unfair the situation is. It doesn't matter if you did nothing wrong. Tell them (in a succinct way) what caused the issue. Make sure you accept responsibility for it. Don't blame, complain, make excuses or otherwise editorialize.

So what do they need to hear? *Specifics!* Each sentence should contain details and be supportive of your thesis, or it should be deleted or rewritten. Here are two examples of root causes, one good, one poor:

GOOD EXAMPLE OF ROOT CAUSE:

"We take full responsibility for our prices, which violated Amazon's Fair Pricing policies. Due to negligence on our part, our automatic repricing program was not set properly and raised prices to the maximum when our competition dropped off the listings for the referenced ASINs. We did not monitor these price changes, and thus charged prices far above the 10% above MAP/average market costs across all platforms."

POOR EXAMPLE OF ROOT CAUSE:

"We have identified the following root causes: We have located the problems in our business which caused the violations in question. Our main problem is that we sourced items in our inventory which are not profitable when sold at the Buy Box price, so we raised prices to compensate for this. We were not aware this would cause problems. We never would have raised prices so high had we known it would violate Amazon policy. The problem was that we were attempting to stay afloat as a business in difficult times, and we are struggling to survive. We are so very sorry."

The first example makes specific references to the issue at hand. It shows that the seller read the policy and is committed to solve the problems they identified.

The second one comes off as a vague apology. It also makes excuses, rather than taking full responsibility. Blaming difficult times, feigning ignorance, or just apologizing is not your best foot forward. These mistakes are very common with sellers and are typical reasons why they end up needing to pay for professional help after a rejected appeal.

In this section, you are basically saying…*I understand why you have flagged me, and now let me show you I understand your reasoning.* I know this may be difficult to embrace but you have to be able to take responsibility to fix similar issues, even if this instance was truly not your fault. But, just accept that this is what Amazon wants you to give them, and then execute accordingly.

THE STEPS YOU HAVE TAKEN TO RESOLVE THE ISSUE

This is your chance to demonstrate that you have fixed the problem(s). Don't make it any more complicated than it needs to be. List out the steps you have taken in plain terms. Your words should convey, systematically, what you have *already done* to fix the issue(s) in question. Assume your audience knows nothing on the given subject matter and walk them through the steps you have taken. The use of bullet points can be very helpful here.

Acknowledge all variables in the equation of your problem. For example, if your issue is product condition, you must address the relevant aspects of sourcing, packaging, and inspection. How has your operation been changed to address the packaging and inspection requirements? What vetting methods did you use for your supplier? Explain your processes for entering products into inventory. If employees were involved, you must include an explanation of how they factored in. You must also reference all applicable Amazon policies. Demonstrate that you've implemented steps that eliminate all the variables that contributed to the original problems. Convince your audience that you have mastered these areas of your business.

Make certain you express the changes you have made as if they have *already* been implemented. Again, you should actually make these changes, as I have already said, *before* submitting your Plan of Action. Do not refer to your changes in terms of actions you *will* take in the future. A successful POA communicates completed action, rather than intention. It shows you are taking active control of your business moving forward.

You should begin to see that your POA is almost writing itself. The foundation you have laid through research and investigation can be built upon with minimal effort. Here are two examples to demonstrate:

GOOD EXAMPLE OF WHAT WE HAVE DONE TO RESOLVE THE ISSUES:

"The corrective measures we have taken to resolve these issues:

- *We have removed from our active inventory all items for which we received fair market price violations.*
- *We have researched MAP and average prices across the web for all ASINs in our inventory, setting our maximum price on every ASIN to no greater than 10% above MAP.*
- *We have applied the Competitive External Price rule to all listings in our inventory, and will apply these parameters to all future listings.*
- *We have ensured all employees are knowledgeable of Amazon's Fair Pricing policy (THIS IS WHERE YOU WOULD ADD THE LINK TO SPECIFIC POLICY, TO SHOW YOU READ IT).*

- *We held an emergency all-staff meeting where all employees read the policy aloud, and were subject to a written test of the main points of the pricing policy, including our methodology for setting our final prices on the Amazon Marketplace.*
- *We dedicated a specific employee to monitor pricing for our inventory, and research all ASINs across the web. This employee compares prices on all ASINs in our inventory to prices across the web using Google, Keepa, Target, Walmart, and eBay. This research takes place once every 24-hour period, including weekends."*

POOR EXAMPLE OF WHAT WE HAVE DONE TO RESOLVE THE ISSUES:

"Greater detail on the actions we have taken to resolve these issues:

We have reread Amazon policy regarding pricing and have adjusted our prices accordingly. We are deeply sorry again for violating this policy and vow never to do it again in the future. We truly believe we should be reinstated, as we hold pricing in high regard and wish to provide excellent experiences for all customers. Our business is dedicated to representing the Amazon brand in every facet of our operation and fair pricing is now our highest priority."

The differences here should be obvious. The first example is detailed and demonstrates the action steps taken. It communicates very clearly that the seller has taken all actions possible to address the violation. The second one is too vague, and reads like an insincere apology. Unfortunately, the poor example in this case reads like many rejected POA drafts clients have shared with me. While the sentiments aren't exactly wrong, this example does not lay out enough specifics, and therefore would most likely be rejected.

I hope you are beginning to understand the difference between a well-written POA which has a good chance of approval and one that is poorly written and will probably fail. If not, read on, and the light bulb is sure to go on!

THE STEPS WE ARE TAKING TO PREVENT THESE ISSUES IN THE FUTURE:

This is where you can highlight how you have put steps in place to keep the issues Amazon notified you about from happening again. What kind of training have you implemented? What new quality control and inspection measures are in place? What processes have you changed? What are you choosing to *not* do anymore? Do you have a new vetting policy in place for suppliers? Did you recall inventory or update ASINs? Is there a new software or service that you've integrated? Have you hired and trained new staff? Have you hired a consultant?

While the Root Cause section of your Plan of Action addresses the present (or most recent past), this part addresses the future. Inevitably, there will be some overlap in what you cover, but I always advise avoiding the temptation to simply repeat the actions you have already taken when talking about future actions. Think of this in terms of our health analogy: as far as immediate action, you cut out fast food, quit smoking, and stopped pulling all-nighters. Future steps involve new habits like exercise, supplements, yoga, and prayer.

Proactive prevention is the theme here. You will want to reference a new understanding of specific policies (always include specific policies by name). For example, if you have read Amazon's Condition Guidelines, refer to that directly. This section can often include the name and address of a new source for products you have found. Mentioning this demonstrates your ability to open new vendor accounts and find additional types of authentic inventory. You want Amazon to know that you are both able and willing to find new sources. Even if a previous vendor was lucrative, you need to be willing to leave them behind if they are the source of your Account Health issues.

As I've already mentioned, you will want to express specifics about your new vetting methods for choosing suppliers. Are they licensed for any specific purpose? Are you able to inspect their facility? Can you check to make sure they are in compliance with their local and state governmental authorities? Can you determine if they have authorization to sell the brand they carry?

Don't overreact to this list of questions. Obviously, not every seller is going to go to this level of research to vet every supplier, even if it would be beneficial. Again, you are using the experience of writing a POA as a catalyst to become a more professional operation.

It is a good time to describe your new employee rules in this section of the POA, as well. You might want to refer to new guidelines added to your employee handbook, or new training procedures. Again, implement these things- if you don't already have them in place-*before* submitting your plan.

Be sure to highlight any new software or processes you have implemented. If you are addressing pricing, you should call attention to the removal of the ASINs in question, as well as all inventory connected to pricing

AMAZON PLANS OF ACTION

issues. Include all relevant details regarding these changes.

GOOD EXAMPLE OF WHAT WE HAVE DONE TO PREVENT FUTURE ISSUES:

"What we are doing to prevent this from happening again:

- *We continuously monitor prices for both online and retail stores (including eBay, Walmart, Target, and Google) every 24 hours. We compare them to prices on Amazon.com to ensure our pricing is in line, or is better than the prices on the other platforms.*
- *We will continue to utilize Keepa on every purchase to see what Amazon's prices have been in the past, so we can price competitively.*
- *If after analyzing retail stores, Big Box ecommerce stores, and Amazon's prices, we find we cannot be competitive in our pricing, then we will not offer that product for sale in our Amazon storefront.*
- *We will ensure that we set maximum prices on every new product listed in our inventory no higher than 10% above MAP and/or average price for the main retailers across the web such as eBay, Google, Target, and Walmart.*
- *Our dedicated pricing employee has but one job-to continually monitor prices in our inventory across the Amazon platform and competitor websites, making certain we are never in violation of Amazon's Fair Pricing policy.*
- *In our efforts to be as proactive as possible, we have initiated monthly, recurring audits above and beyond our daily measures to evaluate pricing across categories and brands in our database.*
- *Any items we discover that are not competitive will be removed from our catalog, or prices will be adjusted accordingly.*
- *We added software which extracts dimensions from actual carrier shipping data. We couple it with supplier and Amazon data. We developed algorithms to identify items and groups of similar items where their dimensional weight results in excessive shipping costs. Any such items where the dimensional weight will cause excessive shipping costs are removed from our catalog if they cannot be sold at a competitive price."*

POOR EXAMPLE OF WHAT WE HAVE DONE TO PREVENT FUTURE ISSUES:

"We have taken the following preventative measures:

It is of the utmost importance to our business that we maintain strict adherence to Amazon policy moving forward in terms of pricing. As stated, we have adjusted our prices accordingly. We understand our mistakes and vow to never make them again in the future at any point. We will make certain that inventory which enters into our system is priced fairly to maintain a customer experience that is consistent with the Amazon brand. We have reduced our prices to reflect the above. Employees have been instructed to adhere to our new guidelines regarding pricing so as to better represent ourselves in line with the policies of your marketplace. It is essential that all employees follow these new rules, or they will have severe consequences. Our prices are a reflection of our new attitude moving forward: customer satisfaction is our utmost goal, and we will do whatever is necessary to make sure the customer is always happy!

Can you see the differences? Notice how the use of bullet points helps to clearly delineate the different aspects of your changes. Also, notice how each point in the first example is specific, and gives the impression that the problem has been addressed from every possible angle. The poor example conveys the correct sentiment, but is missing the details which would make it a slam-dunk. While the second example *might* still be approved, the likelihood is much lower. That is the key here: you want to make it easy for the representative who reads your Plan of Action to say "yes" to you.

ADDITIONAL INFORMATION IN YOUR PLAN OF ACTION

You can go into greater detail in an "other information we'd like you to know" section by including language which didn't fit into the main three sections. Two or three additional, persuasive points should be the maximum to include here. To determine if additional points should be listed, simply ask yourself if Amazon would find the information valuable in making a favorable decision. There is no reason to add extra words if they aren't absolutely necessary. Only include language or points which genuinely support your position.

This is where you would mention you have authorization from the manufacturer, and direct the reader to an attached letter. Or, you could mention that you are the inventor and manufacturer of the product in question, then include your patent as an attachment. Be very selective on what you include, and if you are on the fence, don't include it!

CONCLUDING STATEMENT

This is the time to summarize your exhaustive efforts, and to include your "ask" for reinstatement. I usually recommend a few sentences to reiterate your sentiments, as well as the bottom line of what you are communicating. It can be similar to your introduction, but don't just cut and paste the intro into the ending of your Plan of Action. Take the time to restate yourself in a way that demonstrates you take this whole process seriously.

For example:

"We will not engage in any practices in the future which will violate Amazon's Fair Pricing policies. We consider it a privilege to sell on Amazon.com. We are confident that this Plan of Action addresses the issues that we have caused. The new systems now in place will ensure that this type of violation will never happen again. We hope you will agree and reinstate our ability to sell again."

ATTACHMENTS AND INVOICES

Here, you want to remind Amazon of your attachments and identify all documents by name. You should title the PDFs so they are easy to identify:

Examples:

Patent.pdf
B07ANY409.pdf
BrandApproval.pdf

See the section about invoices in Chapter VII (COMMON MISTAKES AND POST SUBMISSION SUGGESTIONS). Proper invoices (or receipts) are essential for your reinstatement. It is not uncommon for a Plan of Action to be approved, but the overall appeal rejected because of something related to invoices. *You read that last sentence correctly*. If your invoices aren't correct, Amazon will not approve your appeal. For example, your invoices shouldn't say "Sales Order" or "Proforma Invoice" at the top. Amazon only wants the word "Invoice" at the top of the document, period.

CHAPTER VI. CONCLUSIONS

Writing your Plan of Action represents a significant milestone in the life of your business. If approached correctly, it should symbolize a move toward the next level of success. Throughout this guide I have encouraged you to keep things positive, as there really is a great future ahead of you (provided you do the work!). Once you have finished writing your initial draft, take a break and go celebrate with a nice meal before you sit back down to reread your draft. You are close to this finish line, but not quite there yet. Though the writing is finished, your work is not. *Do not send it in yet.* I have more important information you will need before submitting your appeal. So, read on and we will finish your case(s) together!

AMAZON PLANS OF ACTION

VII. COMMON MISTAKES AND POST SUBMISSION SUGGESTIONS

I wish I could promise that if you follow every principle in this guide, you are guaranteed to win your appeal. Nothing is a guarantee with Amazon, though. This guide is meant to give you the best possible chance to win, and I am more than confident in this! There are many reasons why Plans of Action are rejected, and the mistakes which cause these rejections are quite consistent. As with all of the content contained in this guide, the root cause affecting your account might not be properly identified. Below, I address some of the most common reasons I have encountered as to why sellers fail with their appeal efforts. I want to remind you that just because Amazon rejects your initial appeal, it does not mean your time of selling on Amazon is at an end.

FAILURE TO APPLY THE PROMISES MADE PRIOR TO SUBMISSION

Amazon will check your account to verify you've taken the actions you said you have. You won't be able to sneak by with promises you don't intend to keep. I have seen many sellers get into worse trouble by trying to get away with bending the rules and cutting corners when it comes to sticking to their word. If you tell Amazon you are making a change, you need to be thorough and apply the changes. To refer back to our fair pricing case-if you apply the Competitive External Price rule to every ASIN you list except one, that one missed ASIN could be enough to cause Amazon to reject your Plan of Action.

INCORRECT/FALSE/DIGITALLY ALTERED INVOICES

I have worked with sellers in every imaginable state of distress, and the panic is understandable. The threat of losing your livelihood can affect your ability to think rationally. Many times, people contact me in a state of desperation, not knowing what to do or where to turn. I have seen folks make many ill-advised decisions. You wouldn't believe the lengths sellers will go in an attempt to resolve their problems...to the point of downright, dishonest cover-ups.

One of the most common forms of this behavior is doctoring or creating invoices. If you attempt this and Amazon catches you, you will have much bigger problems than a Plan of Action request. I am here to tell you it is completely possible for you to get out of the mess you are in without doing anything dishonest or in violation of Amazon policy. As bad as the situation might be, there is hope. I have been a part of many successful appeals which looked bleak at first glance. Take the high road, and your ultimate chances are much better. **DO NOT FALSIFY OR DIGITALLY EDIT INVOICES.**

One of the biggest reasons sellers lose appeals is due to the fact that there is something wrong with their invoices. For example, a recent client submitted a POA which was accepted, but he was not reinstated because the contact information on his invoices did not match the information on his account. This happens very often. *Make sure the information on your invoices matches the exact details of your seller account.*

Your position is much more defensible if you have proper invoices. If they are incorrect, or you don't have them, your best foot forward is to explain why. Amazon may have grace on you if you explain yourself well, but you do need to address the situation carefully and thoughtfully.

I discuss invoices in more detail in the next chapter.

FAILURE TO BE SPECIFIC ENOUGH

Amazon wants to know the verifiable, actionable, measurable, proactive steps you have taken. It is not good enough to say, "I adjusted prices," when what they want to hear is something to the effect of, "I adjusted all prices in my inventory according to the Competitive External Price rule, while consulting Keepa (for historical pricing), Google, Target, and Walmart to evaluate what is the current fair-market pricing for all ASINs." Specifics win out over generalities.

FAILURE TO ADDRESS EVERY VARIABLE IN THE EQUATION

When Amazon asks for a response or appeal, you need to train yourself to look at a problem in your account from every possible angle, as objectively as possible. For example, many issues with ASINs can be traced back to sourcing. And there is much more to sourcing than just finding and buying products. What methods are you using to conduct your product research? What software are you using? Are you selling wholesale or arbitrage? How often do you buy and in what quantities? Who is creating your listings? Do you ensure your packaging meets Amazon's Condition Guidelines? Are you making certain all of your suppliers are legitimate and authorized?

Approach your appeal systematically, while still making certain you are being succinct. The more thorough you are in analyzing the situation and your processes, the more likely you are to win your appeal. Don't make the mistake of being too narrow, addressing or focusing on only one area of problems and then leaving out other issues which were also cause for concern.

FAILURE TO COMMUNICATE WITH A HUMBLE TONE

If there is even a hint of defensiveness in your tone, your chances of losing your appeal increase dramatically. A contrite attitude increases your chances of winning your appeal. I have covered this multiple times, so hopefully this concept is ingrained at this point! If you don't come to the point of accepting responsibility for your role in handling issues with your account, your appeal has much less chance of success.

MULTIPLE PLANS OF ACTION

Recently, a client came to me after he submitted two different Plans of Action for the same case. After submitting the first POA, he realized he left something out. Instead of waiting for it to be rejected, he "fixed" the mistakes he thought he made and submitted a second appeal without waiting to get a reply to the first POA. This created a big mess.

Sending multiple POAs to Amazon creates separate cases and involves different reps who will likely view things differently. I have heard horror stories from many sellers who have sent in more than one appeal at the same time. It is common for one POA to be approved and the other rejected. This creates a terrible scenario that can take months to resolve. If you don't want to deal with extra hassle, time, money, and stress, do not submit more than one POA at the same time for any reason (unless they are asking for multiple POAs for separate ASINs). Submit the best possible POA the first time, and always wait for a response before sending another appeal.

APPEALS FOR PAST CASES, POST REINSTATEMENT

This is another very common mistake. Once an account-level appeal is won, many sellers revisit the *individual cases* which caused the original problems. What you have to realize is that once you win your appeal, the last thing you want to do is reintroduce yourself to Seller Performance in any way. After the win, everything prior to the case is water under the bridge to Amazon. They are essentially hitting the reset button once your appeal is approved. You definitely want to address new issues that arise, but not those associated with the original case. Inviting Seller Performance back into your account after winning your appeal is like asking an IRS auditor to start their investigation all over again after it's already completed.

ASKING AMAZON FOR CLARIFICATION

Don't ever respond to Amazon with anything other than a well-developed POA! I see this scenario over and over: the seller receives communication from Amazon stating there is a problem which needs addressing. Amazon gives very little information about the actual problem (Note: They will almost NEVER tell you what the problem is). This leaves the seller confused and frustrated. In turn, the seller sends an email asking for an explanation. This always makes the situation much worse.

Why is the situation made worse by asking for clarification? Because Amazon will treat your response as a POA, and will reject it. Once you have a rejected POA, it counts against you in the appeal process. Do not respond to Amazon except by giving them exactly what they are asking for! They are most likely going to give you incomplete information and you will naturally feel frustrated, confused, and even desperate. This is why I wrote the first several chapters. Amazon will hold you responsible to do the research on why problems are happening, and give them the information they want in return. Get through the emotions in any way you need to, but don't respond to them with a request for more detail.

WHEN AND WHERE TO SEND YOUR FINISHED PLAN OF ACTION

Once you have finished your draft, take a break from it. Just step away for a few hours, minimum. Let it breathe. Before you send it, you are going to reread it, but only after taking a step away. When you reread it, chances are there might be some minor tweaks or additions needed. In some cases, these minor changes can make the difference between success and failure.

One of the most common questions I receive is *where* to respond to Amazon when they ask for a Plan of Action. Unfortunately, Amazon isn't always consistent in the channels they use to contact sellers regarding cases. Sometimes they send just an email, sometimes a case or notice appears in your seller dashboard, and sometimes they will contact you with both. Be certain to be consistent in checking all relevant areas of your account for cases, and do not rely solely on your dashboard. I mention that because you need to find the initial notice in order to best determine how to reply. The original notification usually includes details for what method Amazon would like you to use for your response.

Amazon's preferred response method these days tends to be using the appeal button, whenever it appears as an option. I recommend reserving email as a second step if the appeal is rejected after using the appeal button.

If you do send an email, make sure it is sent from the email address you use to log in to Seller Central. Include your attachments, and include the POA in the body of the email, as well as by adding the POA as a PDF. The subject line should read as follows: "*Please consider our Plan of Action for* ASIN *B07XYSZ49.*" If you have more than one ASIN to address in the same POA (or if this is for a suspension), you will want to change the subject line accordingly. More and more cases are being handled through forms and automated systems, so emails are becoming less and less necessary.

For ASIN notifications (not account suspensions), I typically only address one ASIN per appeal, unless there are notifications for several ASINs at once for the same issue. I know it's tempting to want to address multiple ASINs at the same time in the same plan, but Amazon usually prefers an individual case/POA for each individual ASIN, unless they cite several ASINs at once in the same notification.

As far as *when* to send your POA, the most important thing to keep in mind is that you usually have seventy-two hours to respond to the initial request. They will usually let you know if they need to hear back from you sooner. In either case, there's no time to waste. I have seen many accounts suspended after the initial notification because the seller took too long to respond and simply didn't provide an acceptable appeal in time.

WHAT TO DO AFTER YOU SUBMIT YOUR PLAN

This may sound obvious, but the best thing to do after you submit your plan is...*nothing*. My advice is to wait patiently for a response, even if it takes longer than you expect. After you submit your Plan of Action, waiting is a big part of the game. While calling Account Health can be valuable for checking status, it doesn't necessarily make the process go any faster.

There is usually very little you can do to make Amazon respond faster. You can hire an attorney and spend a lot of money. You can try to contact them, reach out to different teams, and attempt to escalate. It is understandable that you want to move things forward and take control of the situation, but impatience can often cause more problems. The best thing you *can* do in most cases is accept the fact that you *can't* do anything more. If you are dealing with ASIN restrictions (instead of an account suspension/deactivation), you should still be able to continue to sell the other ASINs which haven't been flagged. You want to make *certain* everything operates smoothly with your account while you are in the middle of an appeal process. It will not help your case if Amazon finds new customer complaints or other violations in your account while they are investigating you.

At some point you will receive a response from Amazon. Hopefully, this response will be a reinstatement. One of my recent clients had to submit two separate plans for different ASINs within a two-week period, and won his appeals both times on the first try. This is the exception, not the rule because it's not at all uncommon for a plan to be rejected. The norm is at least two rounds of back-and-forth, and sometimes it will be more. It can be a process. If you stick to the guidelines presented here (and get help when needed), your chances are very good, if you remain patient.

WHAT IF YOUR PLAN OF ACTION IS REJECTED?

Often, there is more work to do after the initial plan is submitted. If this is the case for you, you shouldn't fret. Like I said, over 98% of the Plans of Action I have ever written have resulted in success...eventually. Amazon can respond in a number of ways, and there is not a general rule on how they respond. They may simply ask for more information. Regardless of how they respond, keep in mind that every case is unique. Since no two scenarios or accounts are exactly the same, you will want to read the rejection message thoroughly so you can best determine what actions to take next.

If you are denied, their rejection reply usually contains clues as to what your POA was lacking. Making a call to Account Health to review your case and request information you overlooked can be beneficial at this stage. It might require multiple calls to multiple reps to uncover any valuable information, so be prepared. Not all reps are equally well-informed or well-trained, so weigh their suggestions carefully before taking any action.

At the time of a rejected appeal, Amazon often asks for more specifics, invoices, or a combination of the two. This usually happens because you either 1. Haven't addressed all aspects of the root cause, or 2. Need to give additional specifics about what you have done to fix things. Amazon doesn't give away all their cards, so many times the seller won't know all the reasons why they are facing suspension (which again, is why the first section of this guide is so important). Keep in mind, you may have to dig even further before you communicate with them a second time. Under no circumstances should you ever submit the same appeal in response! There's always something you can do to improve your plan.

Escalation is a very popular strategy after a rejection. This works best if your appeal was very close to what it needs to be. Chances are, however, that your appeal was not close to what it needed to be or it wouldn't have been rejected. If your appeal has been rejected and you don't know what to do next, it may be time to call in the help of a proven reinstatement specialist before going any further. I have seen a lot of sellers delay reaching out for consulting until they have absolutely nowhere else to turn. By then, it could very well cost more and take longer. Get help before the problem becomes worse!

Another popular, yet controversial strategy post-rejection is opening a second seller account. Operating an unauthorized second account is absolutely against Amazon policy. Amazon has many failsafes in place to catch those who attempt this. I have seen many sellers lose their selling privileges permanently because of opening a second account. Don't do it! The right thing to do is exhaust all efforts to resurrect your suspended account. Whatever you do (even if your appeal is rejected multiple times), do not be tempted to create a second account.

CHAPTER VII. CONCLUSIONS

If you have followed my recommendations, committed yourself to exhaustive research, kept your communication clear, and made the necessary

AMAZON PLANS OF ACTION

changes to your business, you should be in great shape at this point. If you have applied my suggestions and are still suspended (or denied), you are most likely facing a situation which requires help. Many times this is due to the fact that Amazon has not given you enough information to win your appeal. A one-hour call could save you weeks or even months of time, stress, and lost revenue. Refer to the contact information at the end of this guide, and don't hesitate to reach out.

AMA

AMAZON PLANS OF ACTION

VIII. FINAL CHECKLIST

***When a performance notification from Amazon requires a response beyond closing the listing, don't give them anything other than a well-written Plan of Action.** Become well-versed in all the prewriting steps in this guide before you type a single word.

***Manage your emotional reaction.** It's natural to feel frustrated, deflated, defensive, and panicked when you receive a request for a POA. Before going any further, it's important to relax, gather your senses, and deal in facts, rather than emotions.

***Remember the definition of a POA.** Your POA is not a legal defense, apology, or admission of guilt. A POA is a plan of specific actions which demonstrate to Amazon you know why they flagged you and how you have fixed the problem.

***Know the common mistakes.** POAs that contain fluff or are not specific enough are usually rejected, as are those containing even a hint of defensiveness.

***Become a detective.** Determining why Amazon thinks you are in violation of policy is the foundation for a successful POA.

***Study the communication(s) from Amazon to determine any valuable clues.** They will not always give you information directly, but reread their email/case to dig for relevant details.

***Visit Refunds and Returns, FBA Returns, Feedback, Messages, Product Reviews, Voice of the Customer, and product reviews on other platforms.**

Each of these areas may need to be studied thoroughly to determine root cause.

*Implement the necessary changes to your business before writing your POA. Amazon will check to see if you have already fixed the problem(s) when they read your plan.

*Keep your communication simple. Make it easy to follow along and understand the bottom line of your message. Keep your points clear, brief and specific.

*Write a brief intro to set the tone properly. Summarize your understanding of the case(s) from their standpoint, along with how you have fixed the problem(s).

*Establish the root cause(s). Your exhaustive research will uncover answers as to what the issues are.

*The Steps You Have Taken to Resolve the Problem should be active and specific. Show Amazon you have *already* implemented your fixes. Reference policies, procedures, and infrastructure improvements by name and with examples.

*The Steps to Ensure the Problem Never Happens Again should cover every variable. This section should read differently from the previous one in the sense that it focuses on the future. This section references new habits and future preventative procedures.

*Your concluding statement should be an original summary. DO NOT just cut and paste the introduction! Remember to include your "ask" for reinstatement.

*Make certain your final POA is no longer than two pages.

*Make certain your invoices and attachments have file names that are easy to identify.

*All information on your invoices must precisely match the information on your Amazon account. This includes all names, addresses, email addresses, and card information. It's preferable to have one address and one card!

*Print a copy of all invoices and annotate by hand. Do not alter invoices digitally. Circle the products in question. Handwrite the ASIN and circle and/or write in contact information of both your supplier and yourself.

*Include a minimal number of invoice PDFs. Your audience will not want to read dozens of PDFs and may not even open them if there are too many. Include one, PDF for each ASIN (multi-page if necessary).

*Review common mistakes again from chapter V before you send.

*Send your POA through the appeal button, if available, within seventy-two hours. If there is no appeal button available, send via email, with tracking. Make sure to send using the admin email address you use to log in to Seller Central.

*Do nothing after you submit your POA. Do not email to follow up. Do not open a second seller account. Just be patient and wait for a response.

*If approved, do not appeal past cases. Amazon considers it a clean slate once they grant your appeal.

*If rejected, take the process further. Do not resubmit the same POA. Take your research, actions, and specifics to the next level. Consider reaching out for help from an expert.

AMAZON PLANS OF ACTION

SCOTT MARGOLIUS

Dear Fellow Amazon Seller:

Thank you for taking the time to read this guide. Your investment of time should be well worth it, not only in terms of your current (and future) appeals, but also in terms of the overall life of your business in general. My goal has been to convey valuable information about Plans of Action and the appeal process. This is a culmination of many lessons I have collected from helping hundreds and hundreds of sellers over the years.

Accepting the fact that POAs are a part of doing business on Amazon is the first part of a winning attitude. When cases pop up, you shouldn't be surprised or lose heart. By demystifying the POA process, the next time you receive a request from Amazon, it should not be as daunting!

Every appeal is unique, just as every Amazon business is unique. My goal has been to give you many tools to tackle your POA on your own. Once again, I wish I could *guarantee* a victory for you after you finish this book, but that just isn't possible. Amazon's policies are ever-changing, as is their approach to enforcing said policies. Many times, a successful appeal comes down to the Seller Performance representative who reads your POA. Neither you nor I can control that variable. What I *can* guarantee is that you are now much more well-equipped to win appeals, if you have thoroughly read and applied the principles in this guide. You should now have a much better fighting chance.

Your new skills and knowledge are powerful ones in your Amazon toolkit. After all, when you can win appeals, you will have staying power in this business.

After reading through this guide and writing your own plan, if your appeal is denied, you are not dead in the water. If you need to talk to someone about your POA, suspension, ASINs, or any other issue related to your ecommerce business, please contact us! If you are looking for additional training to help learn more of what it takes to sell on Amazon, you'll find options here: ecomsellertools.com/training.

Thank you for your attention and time...

SCOTT MARGOLIUS
Email: scott@ecomsellertools.com
Website: www.ecomsellertools.com

AMAZON PLANS OF ACTION

GLOSSARY

A to z Claim: The Amazon A-to-z Guarantee is a customer satisfaction guarantee intended to protect buyers from bad experiences by offering a no-questions-asked refund. The guarantee covers timely delivery, item condition, and more. A-to-z claims can count against your seller metrics.

ASIN: Acronym for Amazon Standard Identification Number, which is the unique identifier that Amazon assigns to each individual product

Account Health: This is how Amazon evaluates you as a seller. This includes performance targets as well as how well you are abiding by Amazon's policies. Amazon takes action on these metrics when they don't align with their targets.

Account Health Dashboard: Menu hub in Seller Central which provides data and a visual display of a seller's performance standing on Amazon.com. This is the first location to visit when monitoring your metrics as a seller.

Appeal: Sometimes used interchangeably with Plan of Action. The plan is the detailed written document or language you submit, which is a part of the appeal process. The appeal is the entirety of what is sent to Amazon, which may include invoices, documents, and other actionable steps requested by Amazon.

Arbitrage: The strategy of purchasing items from a supplier (like a retail store) and then selling the products for a profit. This process usually involves taking advantage of differing prices for the same asset.

Big Box Store: Large retail establishment, usually part of a chain of stores. Examples are Wal-Mart, Home Depot, and Best Buy.

Black Friday: The Friday after Thanksgiving, which is usually the last Friday of November. This is typically the largest shopping day of the year in the United States, and the official start of the Christmas shopping season.

Bread Crumbs: Metaphor for clues. Bread crumbs lead you down a path toward a specific destination, which usually involves the solution of a mystery, or the answer to a question.

Buy Box: The white box on the right side of an Amazon product detail page, where customers navigate to add items to their cart. 82% of Amazon sales go through the Buy Box, and the percentage is even higher for mobile purchases. Amazon has structured the Buy Box as a competition between sellers, and this competition is based upon seller metrics, including offer price, sales history, feedback quantity and percentage, Account Health, and much more. In order to "win the Buy Box," sellers typically have to outperform the other sellers on a listing.

CSI: Crime Scene Investigators are often highly trained crime lab or law enforcement personnel who collect evidence from crime scenes. They utilize specific methods and procedures to gather and explore evidence. Their conclusions assist in solving crimes.

Chain of Custody: In the context of supply chains, this means you have a way to verify a product's life-cycle and journey. This is the path your goods have traveled all the way from manufacturer to you.

Commingling: Pooling your inventory with the inventory of other sellers at Amazon's fulfillment centers. Go to settings > Fulfillment by Amazon > FBA Barcode Preference > edit. Then, change the selection to "Amazon barcode."

Competitive External Price rule: Amazon's pricing policy intended to make sure pricing does not vary substantially as compared to prices at other retailers outside of Amazon.

Condition hacking: Attempting to doctor or alter the condition of an item in order to be able to categorize it as new or sell it for a higher price. Typically, this applies to used items being sold as new, and where the seller improves the appearance of an item.

Counterfeit: A term used by Amazon to describe a specific violation by sellers. Typically refers to an item that is an imitation of a product, intended to appear authentic and genuine in order to deceive a buyer. Many buyer complaints can trigger a counterfeit complaint.

Dashboard: A menu on a webpage that serves as a main interface and usually includes organization and navigation within the display.

Drop Shipping: A form of retail business wherein the seller accepts customer orders but does not keep goods in stock. The seller sends the orders and shipment details to either the manufacturer, a wholesaler, another retailer, or a fulfillment house, to have the goods shipped to the customer.

FBA: An acronym for Fulfillment by Amazon. Sellers send products to Amazon's fulfillment centers, and Amazon picks, packs, ships, and provides customer service for those products.

FNSKU: An acronym for Fulfillment Network SKU or Fulfillment Network Stock Keeping Unit. The FNSKU is the way that Amazon identifies a product as unique to the seller that sent it to the Amazon fulfillment center.

HAZMAT: An acronym for Hazardous Materials or Dangerous Goods. This is defined by Amazon as substances or materials that can pose a risk to health, safety, property, or the environment while being stored, handled or transported. These items contain flammable, pressurized, corrosive, or otherwise harmful materials.

IP Complaints: Intellectual Property complaints. This could be Trademark, Copyright, Patent, etc.

Inauthentic: A term used by Amazon to describe a specific violation by sellers, though it is not specifically defined and can be widely and/or inconsistently applied. Inauthentic items may not actually be counterfeit, but there was a reason the buyer was not happy with the product or transaction.

KEEPA: Referring to Keepa.com. Keepa software maintains price histories for products on Amazon. Users can individually track the prices of products. Keepa charts document a variety of historical markers and data for a given product, and "reading a Keepa chart" is a particularly useful skill for Amazon sellers.

MAP: An acronym for Minimum Advertised Pricing. This is the price a manufacturer sets for distributors and retailers. The price cannot be advertised for less than what the manufacturer sets.

MFN orders: An acronym for Merchant Fulfilled Network orders, which are fulfilled by the seller. These are Amazon customer orders for which the seller handles all inventory, customer service, shipping, and fulfillment.

Merchant Fulfillment: Often referred to as MFN (Merchant Fulfilled Network) or FBM (Fulfilled By Merchant). The seller is in control of the entire handling and shipping process. Instead of shipping inventory to Amazon to handle, the seller uses their own resources and sends the items directly to the buyer.

Not as Described: A term used by Amazon to describe a specific violation by sellers. The term typically means the item received by the buyer was not an exact match to the listing title, image, or description on the product detail page.

Order Defect Rate: This term (ODR) is how Amazon measures part of your performance as a seller. Amazon takes into account your A-to-Z claims, negative feedback and credit card chargebacks, and late shipments, and then divides them by the total number of orders during a given period. This is shown on the Amazon Health dashboard.

Pivots: Necessary business adjustments which occur as a result of changing market conditions. These are intentional decisions to move in a different direction in terms of emphasis or philosophy, reacting to new variables or obstacles in your sphere of commerce.

Plan of Action: Also referred to as POA, is how Amazon refers to the detailed document they want to receive from you to explain a specific situation they've identified.

Price Gouging: Charging an exorbitant amount over and above what is considered fair for a given product. While state price gouging laws vary, in general they look at the average sale price (ASP) of an item preceding a state of emergency and prohibit price increases over a certain percentage above that ASP due to the emergency. Price gouging is a term that is not clearly defined by Amazon, and one that can be reinterpreted at any time.

Provenance: Refers to the origin of products, specifically how they were acquired and where they came from prior to the seller's acquisition.

ROI: An acronym for Return On Investment, a performance measure used to evaluate the efficiency of an investment. The result is expressed as a percentage or a ratio. If you invest $1,000.00 in inventory which is then sold for $1,200.00, the ROI would be stated as 20%.

Repricer: Software meant to manage various variables such as buy price, minimum price, and MAP. Repricers allow you to set increments to govern price changes for your inventory, using a set of predetermined rules.

Seller Central: The main location most sellers go to in order to be able to access the seller portal at Amazon. Found here: sellercentral.amazon.com

Seller Dashboard: Main hub and menu for Amazon sellers. This is the first screen you normally see when you login to Seller Central.

Seller Performance: Specific team or department at Amazon dedicated to addressing the performance of Amazon sellers. This is the team you will typically hear from and communicate with when a case is levied against you as a seller. Note: this is a separate department from Seller Support. There are many internal teams that are a part of Seller Performance..

Seller Support: Amazon team or department, which is the first line of connection between Amazon.com and Amazon sellers. This is the department you will usually be connected to when you contact Amazon with an issue or question.

Seller University: A great place where sellers to learn about the rules and best practices Amazon recommends. **https://sellercentral.amazon.com/learn/**.

Sourcing: The process of finding products to sell.

TOS: An acronym for Terms of Service. See: Amazon Services Business Solutions Agreement. This contains most of Amazon's policies for sellers.

Used Sold as New: A term used by Amazon to describe a specific violation levied against sellers. The term identifies an item which was claimed to be brand new by the seller, but was actually in used condition when it arrived to the buyer.

Voice of the Customer: A hub where you can use feedback from customers to optimize your products and listings. From this dashboard, you can review the Customer Experience (CX) Health of your offers, read customer comments, identify product and listing issues, and act to resolve problems.

AMAZON PLANS OF ACTION

ABOUT THE AUTHOR

Scott began his career on Capitol Hill after earning his Bachelor of Science degree in political communication. He ended up becoming the COO for a marketing company, a role he stayed in for 15 years. During that time, he also served as a City Commissioner. Whether it was politics or marketing, he learned that what he really loves to do is solve problems. His success has always been tied to a systematic approach. That has helped him identify pain points, as well as strategize how to fix them.

He started on eBay part time in 2000, and spent many years honing his skills before jumping into the Amazon universe in 2012. He reached the top 25% of Amazon sellers in Q4 of that same year, and hit the top 25% again in 2013. In 2014, he made the top 10%, and he still maintains his Top-Rated account on eBay to this day.

As he developed as a seller, he became passionate about helping others succeed. He also wanted to help them learn from his mistakes. Ecomsellertools was born with these thoughts in mind.

To date, Scott has helped hundreds of sellers with both account health issues as well as big-picture strategizing to grow their ecommerce businesses. He has a 98% success rate with appeals, and he has helped hundreds of companies just like yours reach new revenue heights. Today, he is more committed than ever to guiding you through the unique challenges (and opportunities) of the current Amazon landscape.

Scott Margolius is here to help you win the Amazon game. Whether it is general Amazon consulting, listing optimization, branding, account health, ungating, or any other challenge, ecomsellertools is a full-service consulting group dedicated to helping you achieve the results you're looking for.

AMAZON PLANS OF ACTION